Spotted Owl

by Dee Phillips

Consultants:

Kevin J. McGowan, PhD
Cornell Lab of Ornithology, Ithaca, New York

Kimberly Brenneman, PhD
National Institute for Early Education Research, Rutgers University, New Brunswick, New Jersey

BEARPORT
PUBLISHING

New York, New York

Credits

Cover, © Jared Hobbs/All Canada Photos/Superstock; 2–3, © age fotostock/Superstock; 4–5, © Jared Hobbs/All Canada Photos/Superstock; 6, © Minden Pictures/Superstock; 7, © Arnie Smith; 8, © Jared Hobbs/All Canada Photos/Superstock; 9, © Jenny E. Ross/Nature Picture Library; 10T, © Minden Pictures/Superstock; 10B, © S & D & K Maslowski/FLPA; 10–11, © Jim Zipp/Ardea; 12–13, 14, © Jared Hobbs/All Canada Photos/Superstock; 15, © Bob Upcavage; 16–17, © Jared Hobbs/All Canada Photos/Superstock; 18, © age fotostock/Superstock; 19, © Jared Hobbs/All Canada Photos/Superstock; 20, © age fotostock/Superstock; 20–21, © Minden Pictures/Superstock; 22, © Jenny E. Ross/Nature Picture Library, © Tim Zurowski/All Canada Photos/Superstock, © Stone Nature Photography/Alamy, © Gerald A. DeBoer/Shutterstock, © Matt Jeppson/Shutterstock, and © S & D & K Maslowski/FLPA; 23TL, © DCh/Shutterstock; 23TC, © B. Calkins/Shutterstock; 23TR, © Anneka/Shutterstock; 23BL, © Minden Pictures/Superstock; 23BC, © S & D & K Maslowski/FLPA; 23BR, © Jared Hobbs/All Canada Photos/Superstock.

Publisher: Kenn Goin
Creative Director: Spencer Brinker
Design: Emma Randall
Editor: Mark J. Sachner
Photo Researcher: Ruby Tuesday Books Ltd

Library of Congress Cataloging-in-Publication Data

Phillips, Dee, 1967–
  Spotted owl / by Dee Phillips.
      p. cm. — (Treed: animal life in the trees)
    Includes bibliographical references and index.
  ISBN-13: 978-1-61772-910-2 (library binding)
  ISBN-10: 1-61772-910-8 (library binding)
  1. Spotted owl—Juvenile literature. 2. Spotted owl—Behavior—Juvenile literature. I. Title.
  QL696.S83P45 2014
  598.9'7—dc23
                                      2013008324

For more information, write to Bearport Publishing Company, Inc., 45 West 21st Street, Suite 3B, New York, New York 10010. Printed in the United States of America.

10 9 8 7 6 5 4 3 2 1

Contents

Treetop Chick

It's early evening in a cool, quiet forest.

As the sun sets, a fluffy gray face peeks out from a broken tree trunk.

It's a northern spotted owl chick, and the broken tree is its home.

The baby bird's parents are away hunting in the forest.

Soon they will return with food for their hungry chick.

Spotted Owl Homes

There are three types of spotted owls: northern, California, and Mexican.

All three kinds live in forests where there are many large trees.

The owls usually make their homes in tall **evergreen** trees.

Some of these trees are hundreds of years old.

How do you think the spotted owl got its name?

evergreen tree

northern spotted owl

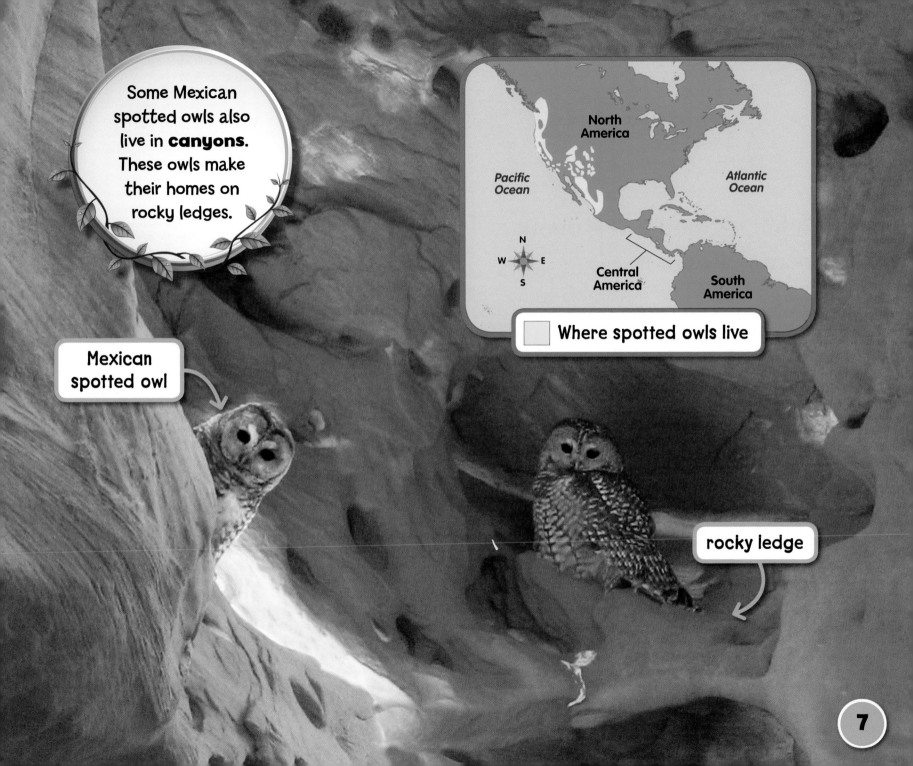

Some Mexican spotted owls also live in **canyons**. These owls make their homes on rocky ledges.

North America

Pacific Ocean

Atlantic Ocean

Central America

South America

N
W
E
S

Where spotted owls live

Mexican spotted owl

rocky ledge

Meet a Spotted Owl

An adult spotted owl is about 18 inches (46 cm) tall.

It weighs from one to two pounds (454 to 907 g).

When stretched out, an adult's wings measure about 3.3 feet (1 m) from tip to tip.

That's about as long as a baseball bat.

A spotted owl is covered with brown feathers. Some of these feathers have white spots, which is how the bird got its name.

Spotted owls hold on to branches with their long claws, called **talons**. In what other way do you think the talons help the owl?

talons

Night Hunter

During the day, a spotted owl rests.

At night, it hunts small animals, such as flying squirrels, wood rats, and mice.

To find its **prey,** a spotted owl sits very still in a tree.

It watches for animals moving in nearby trees and on the ground.

When it spots a meal, it swoops down and grabs the prey with its talons.

flying squirrel

wood rat

mouse

An owl can turn its head nearly all the way around. This helps the owl watch for prey in many directions without moving its body.

An Owl's Dinner

Spotted owls do not chew their food.

Instead, they swallow their prey whole, or tear it into chunks before eating.

Juices in the owl's stomach break down the soft parts of the prey.

The juices cannot break down bones, teeth, and fur, though.

So the owl spits up these parts.

They are all stuck together in a lump called a pellet.

spotted owl pellet

Scientists pull owl pellets apart to study the bones and other parts inside. The pellets tell the scientists what the owls have been eating.

spotted owl eating prey

Starting a Family

In early spring, a male and female owl meet up to **mate**.

They choose a place that will be their nest, such as a broken tree trunk.

The female owl lays between one and four eggs in the nest.

She sits on the eggs to keep them warm.

female owl on nest

A female owl will not leave her eggs to find food. So the male owl hunts for food and brings it back to her.

owl egg

Spotted Owl Chicks

A female owl sits on her eggs for about 30 days.

Then the owl chicks **hatch**.

The baby owls are covered with fluffy, white feathers.

For the first ten days, the mother owl snuggles with the chicks to keep them warm.

After ten days, the chicks start growing thick, gray feathers.

owl chick

male owl

female owl

A father owl brings mice and other prey to the nest. The mother owl eats some of the food. She tears the rest into little pieces to feed the chicks.

Fluff to Feathers

The ten-day-old owl chicks no longer need their mother to keep them warm.

Now, the mother helps the father catch food for their hungry babies.

Soon, the chicks are able to swallow whole mice and other small animals.

After a month, the chicks start to leave the nest and walk on the tree's branches.

five-week-old chick

Growing Up

By the time they are six weeks old, the chicks' spotted feathers are growing in.

The baby owls are also able to fly from branch to branch.

All summer, they stay with their parents and learn how to hunt.

Then, in the fall, the young owls are ready to live on their own.

After two or three years, each owl finds a partner and raises chicks of its own.

six-week-old chicks

A spotted owl's brown feathers help it to blend into its forest home. This makes it easier to hide from enemies that want to eat it, such as great horned owls, eagles, and hawks.

adult owl

Imagine you are a scientist watching a spotted owl family for a day. Write down all the things you see the owls doing.

Science Lab

A Shared Tree Home

The tree where a spotted owl family lives is often home to other animals, such as flying squirrels, woodpeckers, raccoons, and wood rats.

Use paper scraps to make a collage that shows a tree where spotted owls and their animal neighbors might live. Ask an adult to help you find animal photos for the collage on the Internet. Then print the pictures, cut them out, and stick them onto a piece of paper. Include labels that describe how the animals use the tree as their home.

Use the collage shown here as a guide. When you are done, present your collage to family and friends.

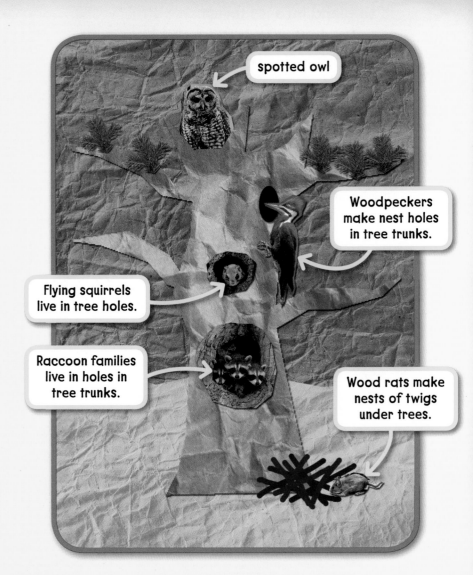

spotted owl

Woodpeckers make nest holes in tree trunks.

Flying squirrels live in tree holes.

Raccoon families live in holes in tree trunks.

Wood rats make nests of twigs under trees.

Science Words

canyons (KAN-yuhnz) steep-walled valleys carved out of the land by a river

evergreen (EV-ur-green) a tree or other plant that has green leaves or needles all year round

hatch (HACH) to break out of an egg

mate (MAYT) to come together in order to have young

prey (PRAY) animals that are hunted and eaten by other animals

talons (TAL-uhnz) the sharp claws of a hunting bird

Index

Read More

Frick, Ivi. *Hunting with Great Horned Owls (Animal Attack!).* New York: Gareth Stevens (2013).

Lawrence, Ellen. *A Bird's Life (Animal Diaries: Life Cycles).* New York: Bearport (2013).

Parker, Steve. *Owls (I Love Animals).* New York: Windmill Books (2011).

Learn More Online

To learn more about spotted owls, visit **www.bearportpublishing.com/Treed**

About the Author

Dee Phillips lives near the ocean on the southwest coast of England.
She develops and writes nonfiction and fiction books for children of all ages.
Dee's biggest ambition is to one day walk the entire coastline of Britain—
it will take about ten months!